If things were perfect (words without frame)

Dragan Jugovic

Copyright © 2022 Dragan Jugovic

All rights reserved.

ISBN: 9798359042734

DEDICATION

To my parents for loving me no matter what I have done, my brother for being always there 4 me, my beloved Firewoman (thank U 4 everything U are), children, my best men, friends and the last but not the least, God, for being patient and keeping me still alive after all these years.

CONTEST

Couple Of Grey Indifferent Trees

Urban Sleeper

Frozen

Release

Suspicions

Sorry Times

Ultraviolet On the Dark Side

Butterfly's Nest

Astronaut

Stripped

Ants & People

Hey, macho!

Creep

Narc

Comatose

Gloves

Her Design

Second-hand Shop Feelings

I've Been High

Undertow

Racism

Mahogany Soul

Masterpieces Fake Design

Tripping Harder

Comes a Time

Dreamt Of You

Frequent

Moonlight Whips

Get Me Upset

Human Garbage Dump

Lucky Messenger

The Wall

IF THINGS WERE PERFECT

If things were perfect
There wouldn't be sacrifice
I wouldn't have to lie

Just look at my face
Like I'm out of space and out of time
Nothing moves but silence across my eyes
Wish I'll never stay without a smile

If I would be good, would you love me more
If I'd be truthful, would I hurt you?

LONER

All my love is gone
I opened many doors with loneliness
Sitting opposite to backdoor, no one crawls in
And it's getting little late to laugh
Silence on my lips
Cold is the kiss

Dark has climb on the wall
No partner for a talk
Have you ever felt like a stone?

(killing) ANGELS

You stepped on the line, you pushed him away
I'm sure he's not conscious
What indifference makes
It doesn't matter if you whip or smile
He wouldn't notice for a long time
But love – are you sure that he's the one

You talk with angels because he doesn't talk
You can fall from the top of the world
And he wouldn't know
But love – is he worth to die for

The less he takes, smaller you feel
Stronger he breaks you, more you give
Isn't it cheap, the last thing to do?
Killing the angel who's runaway
From heaven for you

Love is so strange and you know love can kill
Isolation he makes make you feel you're nothing
And it's not something

So why do you still talk with angels…

FLIPSIDE

Take me to the flipside
Take me on a ride I can't see the end
I'm going to disappear
Somewhere in the cellar of my head

I don't know where I'm going
But I know where I've been
And it all seems so different now,
Looks like confusion
That can turn to accident
Some might take consequences

Flipside, invisible friend
No eyes, no smile, no hands
You'll just feel his weight
Maybe on the table, for the breakfast

Eyes on the wall, its quarter to 12
Soon is midnight and new day beginning
I'm ready to let go another piece of me

THREE GRAVES FOR...

Living in these tribes
Reaching to the sun
Hearing only echoes
Of the silver shining guns
Never-ending Holy Wars
In the name of democracy
Worn out faces of refugees
Promising equality

Raising walls, killing the sun
For women, children and men
Making better kind of gun
For profits, glamour and fame
While falcons flew to the sun
Aren't we just servants for someone's better life

And this entire world will make no sense
When love comes down to nothing

THE SKYWRITERS

Here I am standing on the tallest building
In a couple of months or years I'll touch the sky
Now when I look down, people look so small
Just like their souls are
Traffic jams, cars passing by
No one looks to the sky
Just straight ahead

Looking further in time
I see how we trapped ourselves inside
These walls of our own creation
Making new mankind – zoo nation
But where are the waterfalls and antelopes
Do you still recall them, outside these walls?
Where are the seas, enormous greens?
Where is someone dear?

Hoping to the future
Hoping for something that's away
If we want to make tomorrow
We got to live today

Mother, daughter, father, son
Used to be union, used to be as one
Inside / outside these walls
Machines don't have soul

Standing on the tallest building
I touched the sky ... I died

COLLECTOR OF RAPTURE DREAMS

Cross of silence lies on her lips
No room for something such is kiss
She finds consolation in her dreams

Silent witness sits in her mind
Some stars don't shine so bright
Not so bright like when they're young

Here comes the rain
Is she coming from heavens?
Somewhere away from the sun
Or she comes from her eyes

She's a collector of rapture dreams
And it feels like desert sun
Burns your skin

A-minor FOR BLUES SURFER

See you at the window pane at night
See a man with you, everything seemed alright
Saw you at the street next night drifting alone
Going down the bourbon street to the loser's bar

'This drinks on the house,' said barman
Kill the pain in your soul for a while
Tomorrow's new day and hangover
But you won't lose (feel it) this night
So, take this bottle and cheers
She's your savior tonight

3 am saw you crawl out of the bar
Left some tip to barman to pay for a company
Hey, taxi man, drive these streets
Rest of the night and let the blues play
I'll just lay back in my thoughts
And go nowhere once more again

I'm just another diamond dog
Waiting for the dawn...

INDIFFERENCES

So many things have been beautiful
So many times, I felt unique
Now everything seems so genuine
And everything is already seen

Many differences, lot more indifferences
People keep on building higher fences
Around their eyes, soul and senses...
Outside is cold, people are cold
Making beautiful kingdom far from others
Making beautiful world far from the truth
If I won't be good to myself, I won't be good to you

They wired our souls
Whatever I feel, whatever I say
It doesn't matter, they already know

No more imagination
No more dreaming of someone
No more hiding in the shade of a tree
Love is just an ancient memory

Where has love gone
Where has fantasy disappeared
Where has gone everlasting beauty
Of reflections of the stars in the sea

Distances among the people...
Too many distances

CONFRONTATION

Like a distant shore
Like a home of the whale (and nobody there)
Like a someone who betrayed
Looking at you without a shame...
... Like any falls and its teardrops
When you're down I know you dream on
Can't be daydreaming all your life
Can't hide yourself under and wait for a wonder

Like a dreams of poor
Can easily be blown (in a space between)
Like a beautiful girl
And a man who took your place by her...
... Like unfinished things are always there
Waiting for judgment confrontation
Can't close your eyes and wait for revelation

BRAINWASHED

This night I'm staying in
Don't feel right to go out
Laying on the floor, with my radio
And little creatures creeping along
Sometimes around my legs
Sometimes in my ears
But there's nothing inside to fix
DJ says some stories about infirmities
If you should die before me
I would light the cigarette
I'd be shining ultraviolet

My brain sits in a tin can
I know some of you don't understand
How the rifle can change a size of a man

HARD TO BE A MAN

Reason to continue
Is hidden in me
I come with purpose
To find somebody
Everything's easy
To break like a glass
But it's so hard
When you need to be a man

You fight for ideas
Which are not yours
You're good 'till you're needed
Sold when you get old
Stand in else's shadow
Search source of revenge
Did you ever think
To give a friendships hand?

OUTSIDE THE FRAME

Suppose you get up
And your clothes don't suit you fine
Suppose your morning coffee don't taste nice
Suppose you go outside to job, miss a bus ride
Everything turns upside down
It's not a big deal, it happens all the time

Suppose you find your girl
In a bed with another man
You might say I'm not mad
But deep inside surprised and you pretend its ok
Big deal, it happens all the time

Suppose you found your kid is a junkie
Would you tell him you've been through that?
Suppose you tell him, would he stop?
Suppose he does not
Suppose he tells you "Daddy... Fuck off!"

It's a little guilt in everyone
But I'm not here to judge you
Maybe when you awake one morning
You will be found you're wrong
Then whose better judge than you

Suppose you're a creep supposed to me...

RODEO CONTINUES

Sun is going down, love fades away
Every night I dream of you and you love me
But love fades away...

People are falling down, can't get up
They're not machines, they got feelings
But they push them to fall...

Clock is ringing, time runs out
Rodeo continues, men is neglected
TIC - TAC, time runs out

ON THE CLICHE

With hands in my pocket and down the street
I'm leaving marks of my feet
I see nothing but the peak of my shoes,
When I look around
No one searches interesting things in you
Human profound standstill, it keeps me down

It's easier to ride on the cliché
Live your dreams within'
It's easier to be lazy than change a routine
I still don't believe your points of view
Indifferent moods with dead attitudes
Just listen to yourself:
'Changes aren't good
If they don't come by themselves '

So, nothing's going to change
Because you can't change yourself
And those barricades within' you...
So, step out in the sun, you fuck
Inhale and look to the sky
Don't change direction of
Your eyes to the other sides
You'll find the reasons that are keeping you down

NOTHING CHANGES NOWADAYS

Memory, my only enemy
Hell is 'round the corner
But no one sells a remedy
Shed no tears
Because this fear isn't what it seems
And my brain isn't thinking what I'm saying
No apologies and no excuses
For what we did, done, do

My poor brain exhausted
My poor brain toasted

I'm going to fly right into the sun
Yeah, into the sun, man
Some of you don't understand
Hey fucker, you can be my brother
Be my brother...
When alien becomes human!

Everything's the same
Nothing changes nowadays
It takes so much for a touch
Yet so little to bury a man

Life is everywhere, take a look
On every corner crucified on hooks
Today he's good yet tomorrow so cruel

GOING HOME

I shut my legs off, I've painted my eyes black
Granted wings to my body
Feeling like I'm coming back
I shut my mind off to become a meat on the street
Gallons of horny energy, I feel hunger for me
Humanity on my hands
Too many problems to understand
Jealousy in my pockets, strangers in my accents
You should remember me on that silver silent shore
I adored you but you've made of me a whore

With cigarette in his mouth
Man stands on the sidewalk
Black hat, grey raincoat, rain doesn't stop to fall
Seems like he waits something, taxi or a girl
I've seen that look before and I know how it hurts
He put out cigarette, sidewalks become too small
So, he decided to go a little further
His friend was a business man, his girl was a queen
He splattered their brains out on some highway
And earned a great throne in a prison cell

You should remember my face
Because you ate my soul
You inside my thoughts, I shut myself off
I thought it's my imagination
I thought it's a dream

Someone blew in my neck
I couldn't see anyone here
So, I turn off the lights and I hugged darkness
Now I drink the last cup of my life
And I'll sleep tight for me
Easily I put my head down,
Oh, how it's good to be finally free

QUEEN IN JESUS CHRIST POSE

I exist in your room
Only when you want me to
I'm hanging on the breeze
Only when you breathe
On your favorite liar's mouth, your magical smile
On your dry tongue, your precious eyes

I exist like court jester
Whenever you want me to
You should feel how I feel
I am a commodity
I'm your favorite radio song, I'm your delicious
I'm your precious kisses, everything she misses

I'm part of your life
I'm yours private Pilate
I'm crown of thorns
You're queen in a Jesus Christ pose

ALMOST FULL MOON (kittens)

Almost full moon
Somewhere in the back of her thoughts
She's pulling the curtains down
Cigarette in ash-tray, kitten in her hands
Dark hangs clumsy on the wall
Such a perfect night for being alone

Like this city don't have soul
Like this people are dead inside
Are the ruins, dust and bones
The only thing we'll leave behind

Almost full moon
She's ready to talk to kitten until sunrise
She doesn't mind and that's fine
Hands on her knees, kitten in between
She's afraid, can't see things clear
Just think about your angel, they're always near

COUPLE OF GREY INDIFFERENT TREES

All night long, in the center of town
All night long, me and my thoughts
Like I'm standing on the shoulders of giant
Love like rain can be cold
But rain had never let me walk alone

Small hours gently fade away
Such a perfect morning to get away
In the heart of your arms
Love like rain can be cold
But rain had never killed me so cold

Couple of grey indifferent trees
In big city, just them and me
It's not like it should be
Love like rain can be cold
But rain had never made me insignificant

URBAN SLEEPER

Someone said I can see how you feel
I'm carried away like leaf on a breeze
Catch me now before I go too far

Come to me, world has gone to sleep
Hold me tight, someone broke my dream
Close to flipside, don't let me go now

And I heard you
"Lie down, go to sleep,
I'll kiss you"

FROZEN

Many people passing by
Not even a glance on someone
They just float on
I stand frozen
With million thoughts opened

Has time come to pull out our heads out of bag?
Has time come to feel just what you are?
And I no longer care what you demand

Because life can change in a moment
You can never know what's going to happen
So, it makes me wonder
Do we appreciate every moment?

RELEASE

Like magic butterfly's flight
Under the neon lights
He knows he's going to die soon
But he takes another spin around
I know you'd like that
His flight could last much longer
Just close your eyes
And breathe in life that's around

Like an orphan on the street
Waiting coin besides his feet
And I know he's not here, he's dreaming
And I know he's got to eat
Sometimes someone gives him something
While he whispers thank you

SUSPICIONS

It's no good when you don't want anything
Don't want to live, don't want to die
When even one tear can't drop from your eye,
It's no good when you don't have anything
Don't have love, don't have hate
When you blame everyone but you for your
mistakes

Suspicions in decisions
Creatures of your own creations
Your imagination

SORRY TIMES

Two sisters look like two strangers
Two brothers look like two enemies
That's not the shape of my dream
I'm so sorry but I'm not daydreaming

What can we share if I don't lie to you?
What can we make if I don't trust you?

Cold water sounds, I'm low down
Slipping into something not so comfortable
I'm reaching my hands out
I'm losing the visions of the world outside
But what does it make a difference?
They didn't even notice I'm not around

Who threw the wrecking ball?
Who's got privilege first to fall
Why not me...
There's a hole in my heart
But maybe all I need's
A cigar and cup of coffee

ULTRAVIOLET ON THE DARK SIDE

Young girl in the dirt, ragged skirt
Look away and naked breasts
Saw fear shaping her
And her eyes, ultraviolet
They're on the dark side now
Can't go out the shape she's in
Has to be rebirthed to awake her will

Confused to move on
Afraid to love...
For years

BUTTERFLY'S NEST

Releasing you, defending you
Supporting you, protecting you
Over all – controlling you…

Feeling like a paper doll
Waiting to be burnt out
Gone like a comet star
Wish I knew what I know now

I demand from you to be
For a change – cruel and mean
They are hanging on a leaves
We are waiting you to breathe

ASTRONAUT

Parody, tragicomedy
Disharmony not harmony
Obscene and dissolute riches
Clumsy peasants
Hate, do not love
Fear, do not faith
Materialists, not God
Man, not man

Should I graduate for astronaut?
Fade in outer space
Or should I close myself in a jar
Stay in this place

Every day brings its own disease
Can't love you much as you hate me
You go hungriest every day
You represent yourself bigger than God
Because it's hard to be pure as a child

STRIPPED

Your entire world turned to black
As love cedes place for hate
Army of your so-called friends
Just a thousand still life samples
Reminding you of your own killer
Some things should be sweeter

Pale blue eyes, no romance
Can't you feel beauty of grey?
Nobody tells you how to love
Nobody helps you to get up after fall
Nobody shares with you even a thing
How do you feel stripped?
Isn't it ironic after all you did?
It hurts sure a lot but it's all you feel

ANTS & PEOPLE

Little ant keeps coming over me
Lots of people keep coming over me
I can't crush them like I can smash this ant
Guess it would be cruel to kill this little man
This fellow that I'm waiting to say hello

Living on the edge of the night
Who knows the way we're going to die?
And if you wait too long
Maybe you won't find your way back home

HEY, MACHO!

I never wanted to let you down
But I had to give a scapegoat
It's been hazardous to leave you out there
Because someday you could turn back home

I never wished to leave a sculpture
At the shore out of sight
But how much more you'll lie people
Before they breakdown

He tries just to justify himself
But you won't get a credit, not this time
Supermodels, cocktails, nice try
But not this time, motherfucker!

I got myself and I'm not dead
Not for sale, not for rent

CREEP

Can you sleep like a child?
With secret worlds in your mind
Undiscovered and without lies... well, maybe

Can you tell the truth like a child?
Without hesitation someone can be harmed
Can you say you're innocent... well, maybe?

But why can't you say you're free
Why can't you admit you're a creep?
And with new dawn
Your shadows won't disappear

NARC

When I look at myself
Slowly walking down the street
I feel like a creep I wanted to be
Those high hopes buried in my feet's
What to do, what more to give
I try to think and I try to breathe
And there was that man who didn't want to be...

... This time like any other
But I don't want you to bother
When I'm on, I want all
When I'm down, do not disturb

My hair is dancing with wind in the sky
And I'm myself not who you like
I don't need spies, to see my eyes
Shits in my head, bugs and flies
And I tried to sleep and I tried to breathe
But there was that man who didn't want to dream...

... This time like any other
I know I always bother
When I'm on, I am whole
When I'm low, do not disturb

COMATOSE

Isn't my business
Because driver rolled over the man
Isn't my business who has passed away
Isn't my business to take care for surrounding
Isn't my business to make something from nothing
Isn't my business for the world's decadence
Isn't my business to try to change ourselves

Isn't my business because the wars are around me
Got no time for those who call themselves Pacifists
Isn't my business to clean someone's other shits
Isn't my business to fix relations between people
Isn't my business to glue broken
Isn't my job to keep my eyes wide open

GLOVES

Drowning in my sea
In the sea of my love
If you want me like I you
I have love for both

Triggers inside my head
And pearls around me
You and me, hand in hand
But why are you pretending?!
Gloves on your sweet hands
Touches are so cold
You don't want to take them off

HER DESIGN

She's taking my voice
The same way she took my soul
She feels comfortable in my skin
How do I feel

I shouldn't allow this design
You made for me
I'm not available to be all yours
So sweet
You keep talking, I'm chocking
Can't see myself in these things

SECOND-HAND SHOP FEELINGS

Forward yesterday
Forth and back today
It all comes at my way
I must face it anyway
Everyone I know
Turns to animal
They make a creep of me
They leave it all up to me

Everyone walks like saint
And everyone is thief
Wish I can be their judge
And meet them with mother grief

Somewhere by the mirror lays your make – up
And you're smoking, talking, chocking
Woman, take a break
'Because I don't care anyway

I'VE BEEN HIGH

I've been high but never too much high
Always knew difference between charade and life
I've been here and a little bit there
All this distances always get me somewhere

I've been right and I've been wrong
I won't say I'm sorry because we couldn't get along
I've been honest, I tried to do good
It's not my fault if you couldn't stand the truth

I've been hurt but also loved
Many good feelings
Because silence never stay too long
I've been high… Oh God and I felt so fine

UNDERTOW

Winter in my head can't send away
Can't see nothing under snow surface
Cold I live don't turn to fire
Good things what've been here are hired
Got no use to put the curtain on my eyes

Sometimes, they force you to shift
With empty wallet can't buy a dream
House of brick's easy to build
Smile of concrete's hard to crush
Creeps over my head I tried to trade for innocence
But didn't feel even the surface of it
So, undertow I go
With the perfect girl that you don't know

RACISM

Just like you I am just a man
Don't need racism, don't need hate
I don't mind for your color skin
I just want to live
Only difference between you and me
We don't share same opinion
About irrelevant things

If you hate me, don't look at me
Because I'll start to look at you
And I'll learn to hate you too

MAHOGANY SOUL

All you have, you try to make invisible
All you want, you try to make possible
All you do, you want to do it right
All you feel, you can't hide inside

All your virtues won't be
Truthful if there's no aim
And all your shoes won't last
Enough to get you where you head
All the changes you do
You do to be a better man
And for some changes
You can't prepare yourself

MASTERPIECES FAKE DESIGN

Beautiful people inside the museum
Exhibition is on the highest level
Approval of faces for the masterpieces
And name of the artist's invisible

Perfection of pictures leave breathless
Looking so authentic like they'll never die
Invisible artist watches them from balcony
Their adoration made sadness in his eye

Shaping themselves in counters of pictures
Fitting in frames
Closer, farther, to observe and admire
Someone else sits on their shoulders
Silently making his own design

Invisible artist left museum and parade
And sit on the bench by the lake
Hole in his heart was getting bitter
All the masterpieces were fake

TRIPING HARDER

Some might say they don't see the sun no more
You're part of the night I used to adore
Some might say they've reached the top

Now it doesn't matter who they've been
And some might say it's okay
Making nothing from something
But know they don't know a thing

Why cant you get it right
Why don't you face it like a man
Some might say it's okay to put yourself aside

COMES A TIME

You know it takes a long time
To leave this highway
It's gonna take a piece of mind
To drop a piece of you behind
You know it takes a long flight
From sad lips to wide smile
From unrequited love to beautiful one

All your dreams and fiction
Can't change the truth...
Comes a time to open your eyes
Comes a time to clear your mind
Comes a time to look outside
The world you've created inside

I'm going to grant you a song
A part of my soul
I don't talk about being alone
I talk about love

DREAMT OF YOU

I tried to chase the sun on his way
I dreamt of you, you said let it go away
I wanted to tell you the way that I feel
I wonder where you are now

I speak with clouds did they see you anywhere
I dreamt of you but you made it go away
Show me how I will carry on this way, without you
I wonder where you are now

Lost on freeway, it doesn't make sense
Million cars, I can't no more defense
I dreamt of you but I lost you on the bend
On this way of nowhere

FREQUENT

Bad noises, inner mind mess
Words crushing inside
Can't spit the right ones out of my chests
I'm like virgin, staying on the sidewalk
Fear of losing innocence

Evening silence flows with broken rhythms
One more glance I'll take
Before my feet's fly over my head
Little blink across the sky for the sunset's sunshine

I've never been for you...

MOONLIGHT WHIPS

I'm free falling, gently and slowly
Like a shutting star, so old and lonely
No one's going to catch me tonight
Far from the moonlight whips
Who's tonight so sweet?
Was it angel or you?
Was it just a dream?

I'm human not cold machine
Some things I should let them be
As they are
Until I'm in a sleep

GET ME UPSET

One hundred percent
You always get what you meant
Most of the time, others you just don't respect –
Cause I was around waiting for a smile
'Till you blew my head off
And I was around with your taunting style
I didn't need your scoff

One billion stars, driving in moon cars
But your kiss granted me a scar –
Cause I was around looking for a girl
But I felt like I found a lepper
And I was shining like a diamond in dew
But you made me feel less better

A bullet proof vest, I knew I did my best
But you always get me so upset –
Cause I was around waiting for a smile
But you pulled out a gun
And I was around, aware that I will fade out
Au revoir, so long, bye-bye my setting sun

HUMAN GARBAGE DUMP

Hey, Mister Time, will you give me award
Hey, Mister Time, will you stop the clock
I want to be immortal
I want to see eternity
Hey, Mister Time, I want you right now

Hey, Mister Nice Guy, what is your price
Hey, Mister Nice Guy, how much you're nice
I will pay for pleasure
Just to enlarge your treasure
Hey, Mister Nice Guy, can I get it cheaper now

You can't take it with you when you die...

LUCKY MESSENGER

I'm still dreaming of someone good
I'm still dreaming "People, don't be so cruel"
Midnight has passed, soon is the sunrise
I'm still dreaming

How lucky we think we are
Living these days in this paradise
With blindfold on our eyes
How lucky we think we are

Around your neck is a beautiful souvenir
Can my kisses replace it
Are you beautiful like wild horses
Or you're dangerous like August Pinochet

How lucky we think we are
Living another day in this paradise
In this suicidal tribes
How lucky we think we are

Lucky messenger furtively hovers
Somewhere in my view
I want him to tell us some good news

THE WALL

There's a wall between us
Or it's just in our heads
Call it whatever you want
But we don't want to jump it over
It has always existed in our souls
Kept us stuck, frozen
Never letting us to go on

Many things would be easier
If we dare to crush all the walls
No barricades, frontiers, religion
No riches, no poor, no war
Only love covering the wall

IN THE END

Dragan is currently living in Belgrade

But his soul lives around the globe

The art for front cover is used by the permission of the artist Predrag Bozic.
Special thanks to Mursel Jahic

Instead of biography, people spoke about me...

"He's quite a wispy guy, isn't he! Cheerful - but gets gloomy when someone blocks the sun... Cheerful - loves life and enjoys living it, happy - because he has real friends around him. The point of view determines what you will see, and our he stands in the right place"

"The Hobbit? So dear to all of US. Such a small, sweet, brave, hard-working, smart creature, ready to help everyone when needed, and has gone through so many hardships that life brings! But he always walks forward with his head held high... he is not very friendly - he prefers to stay at home, but when he hangs out, he really hangs out, and how can you not love such a creature!!!

SMALL - *I mean little*

SWEET - *like bonbons*

BRAVE – *gladiator and a half*

WORTH IT - *does a lot of what*

his friends never dream of doing it

SMART - *like a bee with a bucket of honey"*

''That small, cheerful, smiling, strange man radiates incredible positive energy, ... and while we listened, he read ... while we played, he wrote ... while we celebrated, he basically "rested" ... cool and calm, and at the same time live and high ... I really trust him immensely ...''

''In short, what I would say about you is that most of my super stupid things (the best ones) are related to you. You always supported all my antics and meanness! And of course, afterwards you had to expiate all my confessions! Love you!''

''Thus, one wonderful sunny day, on the planet ''Badia'', in a circle of naked butts, I met a little hobbit, who became my best friend. Day by day our friendship grew... that little hobbit was even involved in a love tangle, which, again thanks to that same hobbit, fortunately, could not have ended better. That hobbit has a lot of good sides, but also some ''bugs''. Good, hardworking, funny, interesting, nice eyes, with an apple butt, hyperactive when he drinks one, 2, 3... beers or bottles, a real friend, generous, not an alum, excellent bassist, drummer, keyboardist, guitarist, percussionist, excellent dancing butt, persuasive, scheming, stable, sticks to his word and decisions, lies a little, steals a lot, first-class jerk, whatever you ask him, he has an answer, a lid to every pot and I love him so much!''

www.ingramcontent.com/pod-product-compliance
Lightning Source LLC
LaVergne TN
LVHW050344160826
845677LV00014B/3781
9798359042734